Asia

MONGOLIA

Europe

Africa

Australia

PACIFIC

OCEAN

CEAN

MONGOLIA
VANISHING CULTURES
Jan Reynolds

Harcourt Brace & Company

San Diego   New York   London

Requests for permission to make copies of any part
of the work should be mailed to: Permissions Department,
Harcourt Brace & Company,
8th Floor, Orlando, Florida 32887.

Library of Congress Cataloging-in-Publication Data
Reynolds, Jan, 1956–
Mongolia : vanishing cultures/by Jan Reynolds.
p.   cm. — (Vanishing cultures series)
Summary: Two nomadic Mongolian children listen to stories of the
past from their father and yearn for their own horses, creatures
essential to their way of life.
ISBN 0-15-255312-6 — ISBN 0-15-255313-4 (pbk.)
1. Mongols — Social life and customs — Juvenile literature.
[1. Mongols — Social life and customs.] I. Title. II. Series.
DS19.R48   1994
951.7′3 — dc20   93-1351

First edition
A B C D E   A B C D E (pbk.)

Printed in Singapore

To Bonnie and Tim
for giving life to my vision,
and to all those who share
the vision around the world
—J. R.

To take the photographs in this book, the author used
a Nikon N90 with 20mm, 35mm, 105mm, and 180mm lenses.
The display type and text type were set in Palatino by
Thompson Type, San Diego, California.
Printed and bound by Tien Wah Press, Singapore
Production supervision by Warren Wallerstein and Kent MacElwee
Designed by Lori McThomas and Camilla Filancia

Mongolians live in the heart of the Asian continent, in a land of high mountains, lush grasslands, and harsh desert. They raise and train strong horses, which they ride to herd cows, sheep, and goats. They live in simple, round houses they can easily take apart and pack up into loads to be carried by their horses and camels. They move often, traveling from place to place in order to find fresh green pasture and plenty of water for their animals.

But this ancient way of life is disappearing. Roads for trucks are being built across the country and permanent buildings constructed. Life is changing for Mongolians as their horses and portable homes are replaced.

Because they spend their days on the plains with their livestock, the Mongolian herders believe their own human spirit is connected to the land and the animals. Nature teaches them her ways of weaving together all life on earth. We are all part of the same human family, connected in spirit to the earth. Perhaps we should take a look at the Mongolian way of life, learning from nature, before it vanishes forever.

As the evening clouds sweep over the great plains of Mongolia, Dawa asks his father to tell him and his cousin Olana one more story.

Dawa and Olana listen to Father's tales late into the night.

"Long ago your grandfather was given a young, high-spirited horse by his father. He cared for the horse and trained it to carry him like the wind across our wild plains. Mongolian horses are known far and wide as the swiftest and strongest of horses."

The candles burn down lower and lower as the night grows old. Dawa and Olana fall asleep dreaming about having horses of their own.

The next morning, Father saddles up a horse for Dawa to use, and ties it outside the cluster of *ger*s, round portable huts made of wood, felt, and canvas. Dawa's family and Olana's family always keep their gers next to Grandfather's. They all live together as one extended family, out on the land through the changing seasons, close to nature.

Father rides out to bring in the herd of horses the family owns. He wants to find two small horses for Dawa and Olana.

The boys wait impatiently for the horses, while Olana's father tells them how important it is to have a well-trained horse. The family uses the horses to help round up the cows, goats, and sheep that provide them with meat, milk, leather, and wool.

While they talk of horses, Olana's mother is inside her ger, heating milk over the stove so she can make yogurt for the whole family, everyone living in the three gers.

Now it is time for Dawa to ride out to meet his father and help herd the horses up toward the gers. But first he needs some help untying the horse.

Father has had his eye on a colt, or a young male horse, for Dawa, and when he is close enough, he stretches forward with a long pole and rope to catch the horse.

Uncle also rides through the herd, searching for a colt for Olana. These two young horses will be trained to help the boys in their daily work.

But for now Dawa and Olana must share a horse, and it is time for Olana to ride with his father to bring in the cows to be milked.

Dawa and Olana chase after the frisky calves and herd them to the pen. Dawa's mother lets the calves nurse before she and her sister begin the milking. They milk at dawn and dusk every day.

After the milking is done, Olana's mother walks the fields picking up dried dung from the horses and cows. Because Mongolians use what nature provides, nothing is considered waste. This dung will be burned in the stove for cooking and heating. Dawa helps by flattening fresh dung to dry it.

Olana knows that the sheep and goats will soon be herded to the gers, so he calls the dog over to help. The dog is useful in their work, but he is also for protection, to tell the family when anyone comes near the gers.

Dawa and Olana wait for the animals to come close so they can chase the goats into the milking pen. Then Dawa's father can catch a fat sheep for the family to have for dinner, and for several dinners to come.

The time has come to move. The family packs up the gers into bundles and loads them onto camels or a horse-drawn cart. They usually travel about twenty miles, moving every month or so to make sure they have fresh grass and water for their animals. In winter they gather together with other people and build a fence around their many gers to protect them from the blowing snow.

At the new home site, Grandfather fixes the roof, while Olana and his father knot the round wooden frame together.

Everyone needs to help put the roof poles into place. Dawa's mother attaches the poles to the walls, which strengthens the ger against the wind.

Pressed animal hair, or felt, is wrapped around the frame and covered with canvas for warmth and protection from the rain. Dawa is glad to have *aaruul*, sweet cheese, drying on the roof again, so that he can sneak a treat when he is hungry.

In the new pasture the animals have plenty of fresh grass and water to keep them strong and healthy.

Other Mongolians in the area come by to invite the family to a large celebration. These neighbors are very pleased with their herd of horses, especially the young ones. Dawa loves to see the young horses that have been brought together for branding—marking the horses with the same pattern as the rest of the herd. This family's mark is a triangle and will remain on the horse for life.

During the celebration the men ride some of the stallions, or male horses, that have not been trained. These horses buck and kick, trying to throw off their riders. The men compete to see how long each man can stay on the horse.

When the riding is over, everyone gathers in the host family's ger to sing and eat. The host, the owner of the branded horses, offers *koumiss*, fermented mare's milk, to drink and gives thanks for the healthy horses that they all depend on. Like many Mongolians, he has learned that he is part of nature, connected by the spirit of life to the pastures, the sky, and the horses.

Dawa and Olana are very pleased and proud to have their own young horses to train, too. They want to ride like the wind across the plains just as their grandfather has, and as Mongolians have for as long as anyone can remember.

Late one evening my Mongolian friend Amera brought me to a small cluster of gers to meet some friends of his. In the soft candlelight, a huge round wash pan of boiled mutton was placed on a stool and everyone gathered around. One robust gentleman handed me a large knife that glimmered in the candlelight and motioned for me to begin. Not quite sure of myself, I started to hack at the greasy meat and everyone howled with laughter. I was neither schooled nor adept at their art of meat carving, and they took over for me, giving me some choice pieces, dripping with fat.

After mastering a few handy words in their language, including *te* and *ugu*, yes and no, the family invited me to stay with them and spend some days with their boys Dawa and Olana. I have found that small attempts to learn others' customs go a long way toward your acceptance by them. Perhaps these simple acts demonstrate your willingness to adapt to, if not understand, their ways and show *your* acceptance of them.

I woke before sunrise as Genma, Dawa's mother, stoked the stove with dried dung to make a small but blazing fire to dispel the chill in the ger. Then she went out to milk the cows with her sister, while the rest of us waited for the air in the small round room to warm. Soon Dawa was up and Genma was back with fresh milk for morning tea. Dawa and Olana took me with them wherever they went during the time of my stay. And it was through sharing their play and chores that I became comfortable with and appreciative of the rhythms of Mongolian life.

These rhythms have existed in much the same manner for thousands of years, long before Dawa and Olana were born. Traces of primitive man in Mongolia have been found dating back 300,000 years, but it was actually the Hunnu people who founded the first proto-Mongolian state. From excavations it has been determined that most all Mongolian arts and crafts have their roots in Hunnu culture and that Hunnu fashions, games, and customs became the basis of Chinese culture as well. One famous distinguishing Hunnu trademark is arrows with whistling tips.

Mongolia came into its own during the 1200s, under the rule of the great Ghenghis Khan, becoming the largest continuous land empire the world has ever known. The Mongols controlled everything from China to Europe. Daily life for Mongolian nomadic herders at that time was quite similar, by all accounts, to that of their descendants, today's herders.

Mongolia has a rich, varied topography and is teeming with exotic wildlife. Bordered by the mysterious Gobi desert, the Altai mountains loom large and rocky in the southwest and are home to antelope and musk deer, as well as the snow leopard. In the east, on the lush, grassy steppes, live wolves and bear. And across the skies above them all soar beautiful hawks, eagles, and falcons, searching for prey.

Nearly two hundred years ago Mongolia began setting aside tracts of land for preservation and today has thirteen nature reserves, impressive when you consider that the entire country still has almost no highways. Perhaps because of their interdependence with nature, Mongolians have long been aware of the value of maintaining all living things in their original environments. They are by nature preservationists.

For Dawa and Olana's family, life centers on the raising, training, riding, and trading of horses. Even though the other domesticated animals provide food, leather, wool, and felt, horses are the backbone of this nomadic culture. The horses, along with camels, carry loads and draw flat wagons bearing the family's total possessions: the ger packed in bundles, the stove, and a few other belongings. Dawa and Olana's family caravans with the herd, traveling about twenty miles at a time to find fresh pastures, pools, and streams to sustain their animals.

Days begin and end with the milking of cows. During the rest of the day, saddles are made or repaired, milk is made into cheese or yogurt, and animals are herded, traded, or prepared for food. As well as going to planned celebrations, people often spend time visiting friends and relatives in their gers, and consequently much tradition has developed around these visits.

When I went with Dawa and Olana to the great celebration of the branding of the young horses, they showed me that I must not step on the threshhold of the ger when entering because it is considered the equivalent of stepping on the neck of the host. As we arrived, koumiss was offered around for all to drink from a common bowl, and snuff was shared from gorgeous hand-carved stone bottles. Guests are expected to sit to the right of the host, but for this celebration the ger was so full of merrymakers that we sat where we could and spent the night like singing sardines.

The day after the celebration, as I waited for Amera to take me back, I sat outside marveling over the fantastic landscape, an unending piece of nature's artwork not yet cluttered by roads, telephone wires, or buildings. While I watched Dawa and Olana leading their horses to tie them in front of the gers, their grandfather came to sit with me. Through gestures and a few simple words, and with Amera's translation help, the grandfather conveyed to me that all I was seeing was his great teacher in life. By working day to day out in the open, he had learned that everything—the land, the animals, his life—is connected. And so, I thought, a herdsman comes to know the spirit of life, by himself, at the hands of the greatest teacher of all.

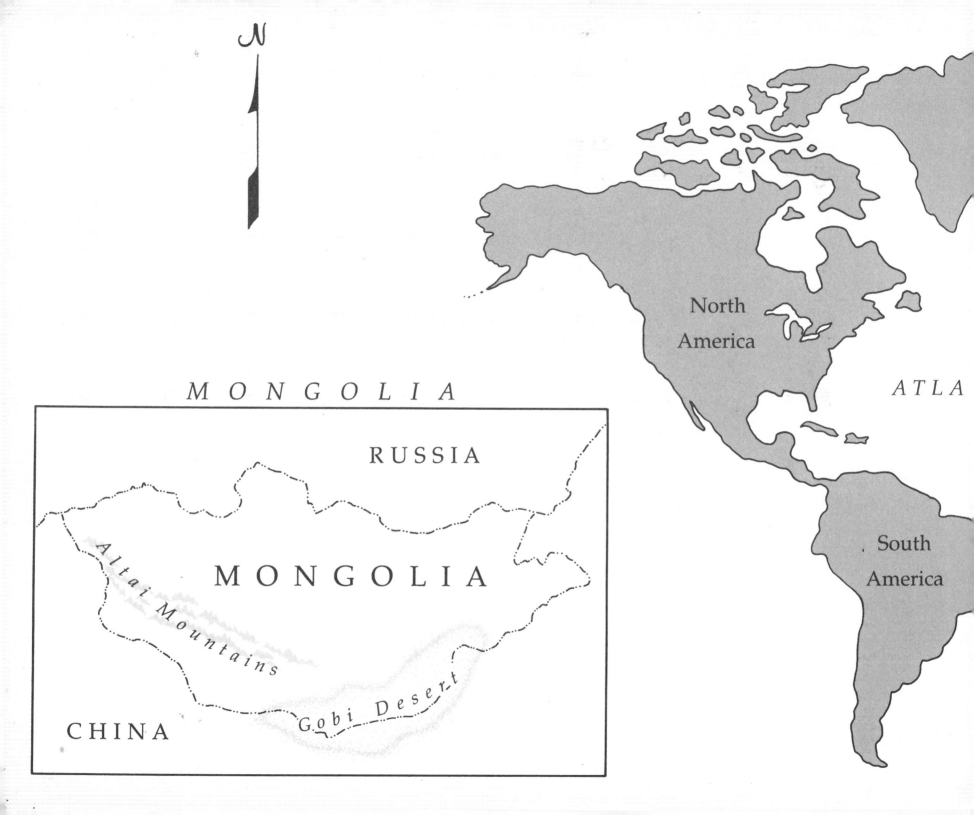